WATER
SUPPLY

James Nixon

FRANKLIN WATTS
LONDON • SYDNEY

First published in 2009 by
Franklin Watts
338 Euston Road
London NW1 3BH

Franklin Watts Australia
Level 17/207 Kent Street
Sydney NSW 2000

Copyright © 2009 Franklin Watts

ISBN: 978 0 7496 8410 5

Dewey classification number: 363.6'1

A CIP catalogue record for this book is available
from the British Library.

Planning and production by Discovery Books Limited
Editor: James Nixon
Designer: Ian Winton
Illustrations: Stefan Chabluk and Keith Williams
Commissioned photography: Bobby Humphrey

Photographs: Corbis: p. 12; Getty Images: pp. 9 top (Paul Harris), 15 top (Travel Ink), 17 top
(Joel Sartore), 17 bottom (Kim Steele); Istockphoto.co: pp. 6 top (Gerald Bernard), 6 middle
(Ryan Ruffatti), 8 (Matt Tilghman), 10 top (Sylwia Horosz), 10 bottom (Silvia Jansen), 18 top
(Marina Lohrbach), 18 bottom (Paul Maguire), 20, 24 (Bill Grove), 25 top, 27 bottom (Lubos
Paukje); Science Photo Library: pp. 9 bottom (Bob Gibbons), 25 bottom (Robert Brook), 26
(Robert Brook); Shutterstock: pp. 6 bottom, 11 (Andrey Shchekalev), 21 top (Elena Elisseeva),
21 middle (Mandy Godbehear), 22 top; Thames Water Utilities Ltd: pp. 13 bottom, 14, 19 top,
23 top; Viridor Waste Management: p. 23 bottom.

Cover photos: Bobby Humphrey: bottom right; Edison Mission Energy: top; Istockphoto.com:
title background; Thames Water Utilities Ltd: bottom.

Printed in China

Franklin Watts is a division of Hachette Children's Books,
an Hachette UK company.
www.hachette.co.uk

Contents

Words in bold are in the glossary on page 28.

Water, water, everywhere

Water is one of the most important things in your life. Every day you need to drink several litres of it. Without water nothing could live. It is in all of your drinks and your food.

We wash ourselves with water. We wash the clothes we have worn and the dirty dishes, too.

Water is always there when you need it. All you have to do is turn on a tap. So where does this supply of water come from?

From rain cloud to tap

The water we use comes from rain. It is the same water that flows in lakes and rivers. It is also present in **groundwater** – rain that has soaked into the ground and become trapped. This book will tell you how the water is collected, cleaned and supplied to the taps in your home.

The water cycle
Water on our planet doesn't just stay in one place. It is constantly moving in a cycle from one place to another (see below).

3. Up in the sky the water vapour cools back into tiny liquid droplets that form clouds.

4. The droplets fall back to the ground as rain.

Sun

2. The water turns into water vapour and rises into the air. This is called evaporation.

5. Rainwater flows into rivers which carry it back to the sea.

1. Water in the oceans, rivers and lakes gets heated by the Sun.

Collecting water

About three-quarters of our planet is covered in water. But most of this water is seawater, which is too salty to drink.

The water we drink is **fresh water**. It comes from rivers (below), lakes, streams and underground. Fresh water makes up only around three per cent of the world's water. Water companies collect this water and pump it via pipes to a treatment works.

Fresh water

Reservoirs

We use reservoirs to collect and store a lot of our water. These are made by building a dam (below) across a river to hold the water back. By storing water in huge reservoirs there is always water ready to use, even when it hasn't rained for a while.

▶ **This reservoir is in the Elan Valley in Wales. It supplies drinking water for the city of Birmingham.**

Drilling for water

Water in underground lakes, called **aquifers** (left), can be collected by drilling deep **wells** called boreholes. The water is then pumped from the boreholes up to the surface. Find out where the water company gets your drinking water from. Does it come from a lake or from under the ground?

Dirty water

The water collected needs to be treated. As rain falls and lands on the ground it picks up mud and germs. If you drank the untreated water it could make you seriously ill.

Polluting water

Water is also made dirty by human activities. Farming and other industries use **chemicals** that can spill into rivers and become part of the water cycle.

◀ **Chemicals used by farmers can run off fields into rivers.**

Before it arrives at your tap, water must be made safe to use and drink.

Making it safe

The government has strict laws about the treated water supplied to your tap. It must meet high safety standards. It should not have an unpleasant taste or smell either.

How water is treated depends on where it came from. River water (above) usually needs more treatment than groundwater for example. This is because it is open to the air and **pollutants**.

Treating water

At the water treatment works, the water first passes through a set of big screens. These act like sieves. They trap bits, such as litter, leaves and twigs. These are then removed from the water.

Adding chemicals

Next, smaller dirt **particles** are removed. Chemicals are added to the water that attract the dirt particles. This causes them to clump together and sink slowly to the bottom of the water. The dirt builds up to form a layer of **sludge** which can be taken away to a **landfill site**.

Filtering

After this, there are still even finer particles that need to be filtered out of the water. This is done by sending the water through a layer of sand and **carbon**.

A chemical called chlorine is then added in small amounts to kill any germs remaining in the water. Chlorine is the same chemical used to keep swimming pools clean.

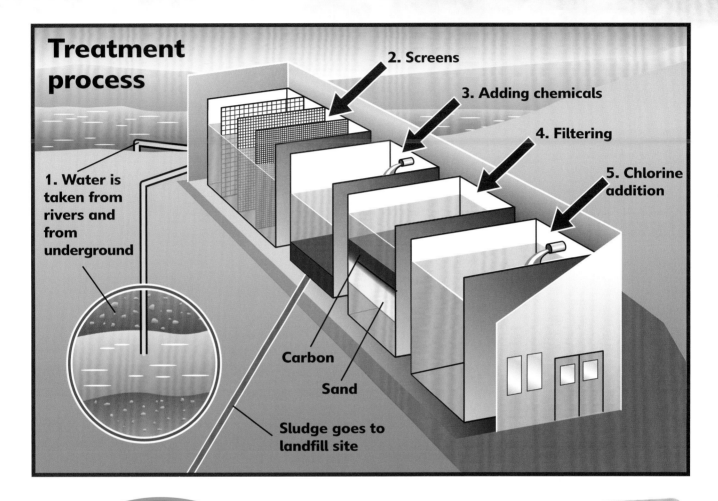

Treatment process

1. Water is taken from rivers and from underground

2. Screens

3. Adding chemicals

4. Filtering

5. Chlorine addition

Carbon

Sand

Sludge goes to landfill site

My name is Anna
Once all the bits are removed it is my job to make sure your water gets **disinfected** properly. After the chlorine has been added, I run tests on the water to check that it is safe to send to your home.

Getting it to you

Treated water then flows into large pipes called trunk mains. They travel underground, carrying the water to homes, schools and workplaces. Mains water pipes can be up to one and a half metres in diameter.

My name is Ben
My job is to repair water pipes that are damaged. Mains pipes run in pairs, so if I am doing **maintenance** work on one pipe, or if a pipe bursts, there is still a supply of water from the other pipe. Sometimes old pipes need completely replacing.

Storing water

Water from the mains is stored in water towers (right) or huge underground tanks called service reservoirs (below). This is to ensure that there is always plenty of water available. From there, water travels through smaller mains into the network of pipes in our towns and villages.

Through the pipes

Water can travel through the pipes naturally by **gravity** if the pipes are running downhill. In flat areas pumping stations are used to keep the water moving along. The whole journey from the treatment works to your home can take as long as a week!

Service reservoir

In the home

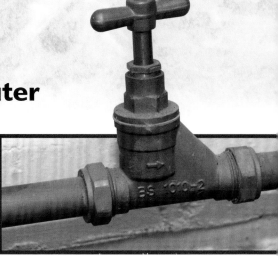

Your water supply leaves the water mains under your street and branches off down a pipe that runs into your home. Where the water enters you will find a stopcock (right). Turning this switches your water supply on or off.

Plumbing

How does water flow around to all the parts of your home? Water from the taps used for drinking and cooking usually comes straight from the mains.

Water going to the toilet, bathroom and hot water tank usually comes via a cold water tank.

Cold water tank

Cold water pipes

Toilet

Bath

Hot water tank

Kitchen tap

Hot water pipes

Stopcock

Mains water pipe

Sewer pipe

Stopcock

There are also pipes leading to your shower and washing machine. The system of pipes in and around your home is called the plumbing.

My name is John

I am a plumber. I go to people's homes to install new water pipes and fix any leaks or other problems with their plumbing.

Pipe protection

Freezing water expands when it turns to ice. If your pipes freeze in winter they can burst open and flood your house. To stop water pipes freezing they are covered with a thick layer of **polystyrene** (right). This is called **insulation**.

Turn on the tap

The water in pipes is under pressure. So how does a tap stop water flowing out all of the time?

When a tap is turned off a little rubber **washer** seals the hole shut. As a tap is turned on the washer moves away from the hole and water flows.

Flush it away

The toilet in your house uses up large amounts of water.

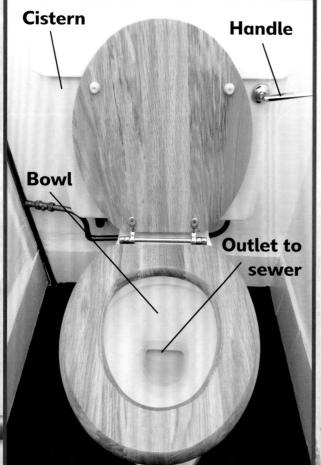

Cistern

Handle

Bowl

Outlet to sewer

The tank, called a cistern, on top of your toilet is full of water (left). Every time you flush, the cistern empties its water into the bowl of the toilet to wash away the waste. The cistern then fills back up with water again.

Water suppliers

There are over 20 companies that supply water in the UK. The company you use depends on where you live. If you live in Glasgow it is Scottish Water. In London it is Thames Water. Thames Water supplies water to around eight million people and has over 100 water treatment works.

Bills and meters

Using water costs money. The water you use is charged for in one of two ways. Either a fixed amount is paid for the year, or bills are sent for the amount of water you have used. Many homes have a water meter, which measures exactly how much water has come into your home.

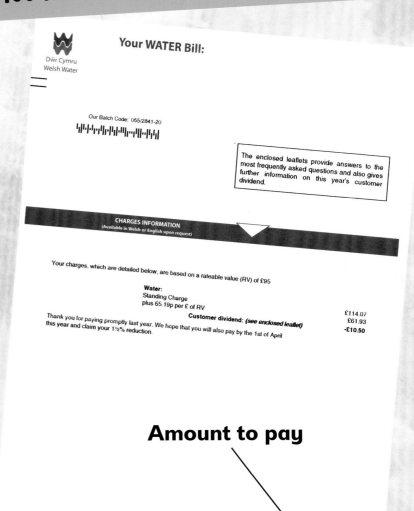

Your WATER Bill:

Dŵr Cymru
Welsh Water

Our Batch Code: 055/2841-20

The enclosed leaflets provide answers to the most frequently asked questions and also gives further information on this year's customer dividend.

CHARGES INFORMATION
(Available in Welsh or English upon request)

Your charges, which are detailed below, are based on a rateable value (RV) of £95

Water:
Standing Charge
plus 65.19p per £ of RV

Customer dividend: (see enclosed leaflet)

£114.07
£61.93
-£10.50

Thank you for paying promptly last year. We hope that you will also pay by the 1st of April this year and claim your 1½% reduction.

Amount to pay

www.dwrcymru.com

For account enquiries
☎ 0800 052 0145 ☎
Mon - Fri 8.00am - 8.00pm
Sat 8.30am - 1.30pm
For water and sewerage service enquiries, please see overleaf

Total Amount Due

£165.50

Precious water

Using less water reduces bills for people with water meters. There is another good reason to save water. The amount of fresh water in the world will always stay the same, but as the number of people living on Earth increases there will be less water to go around.

Droughts

We are very lucky to be able to turn on a tap and get clean water. Poorer countries do not have a network of pipes and water treatment works. Water is collected from wells instead. In some dry areas safe drinking water is in short supply. A major **drought** can lead to disaster.

Even in the UK there can be a shortage of water if the weather has been very dry. Sometimes water companies introduce a hosepipe ban to stop people using large amounts of water.

Here are some ways to stop wasting water:

- Use a watering can (right) instead of a hose to water your plants.

- Use a bucket and sponge to wash your car instead of a hosepipe (below).

- Don't leave the tap running while you brush your teeth or wash your face.

- Have quick showers, not deep baths.

- Don't use a washing machine until you have a full load (right).

Down the drain

When water disappears down the plughole in your bath or sink, or is flushed down the toilet, where does it go?

Dirty water is carried away down waste pipes and drains (left) that go underground. Waste water is called **sewage**.

Going underground

Underground, the sewage travels into great big pipes called sewers, where it mixes with waste water from other houses and factories.

The sewer system is a massive network of underground pipes. It takes all the dirty water to the nearest sewage works to be made clean and harmless.

Sewage workers make sure the sewers are working properly (right). They get down to the sewers by climbing down through manhole covers in the street.

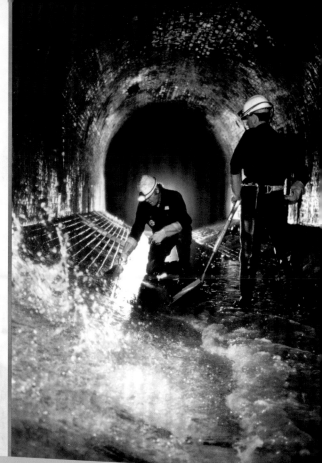

Septic tanks

In some parts of the countryside homes are not connected to the sewer system. Waste water flows into a septic tank in the ground instead. Liquid waste gradually seeps out of the tank and drains away into the soil. The solid waste left over is removed from the tank by a tanker once or twice a year and taken to the sewage treatment works by road.

Cleaning the waste

By the time sewage gets to a sewage treatment works the water is a filthy soup. It will have picked up food waste, sand, oil, chemicals and even rubbish, such as rags, wood and plastic.

Removing the rubbish

The cleaning process at the sewage works is very similar to the treatment of water before it gets to our homes (see pages 12–13). The first stage is to screen out the big chunks of rubbish using a large strainer. Then the sand, grit and stones are removed as they settle to the bottom of the water. This will prevent the cleaning machinery being damaged later on in the treatment process.

Removing the dirt

Next, the waste water rests in settlement tanks (below) where any solids sink to the bottom to form a sludge. The sludge can then be removed. Any grease or oils rise to the surface and can be skimmed off.

Finally, the liquid is trickled over a circular bed of stones (left). The stones have **bacteria** on them, which eat up and filter out the remaining dirt in the water. The treated water is now much cleaner and completely harmless.

Back to earth

What happens to your waste water once it has been treated?

Disposing of the sludge

The removed sludge is **toxic** and has to be dealt with carefully. It is put into a digestion chamber where it is heated at a high temperature to reduce the sludge and kill off the germs. The sludge stays in the digester for nearly three weeks. After this the sludge is safe enough to dispose in landfill.

Fertiliser

The sludge can also be treated and made into a fertiliser. Farmers spread it over their land to make their crops grow better.

Back in the cycle

The water that has been cleaned at the sewage works is safe enough to pour back into the seas and rivers – the same place your tap water came from in the first place!

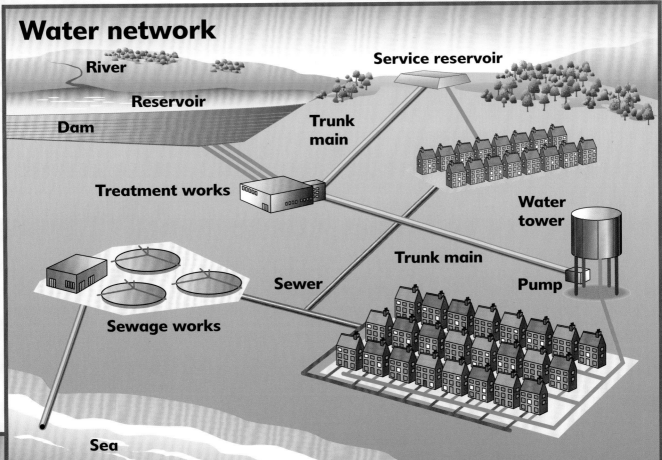

Water network

River

Service reservoir

Reservoir

Dam

Trunk main

Treatment works

Water tower

Trunk main

Sewer

Pump

Sewage works

Sea

The water that went down your plughole becomes part of the natural water cycle once again. It could be collected and supplied back to your home many times!

Glossary

Aquifer A body of rock that contains or transmits groundwater.

Bacteria Microscopic living things.

Carbon An element found in charcoal and coal.

Chemicals Substances that have usually been created by people.

Disinfected Cleaned with a chemical in order to destroy bacteria.

Drought A long spell of very dry weather.

Fertiliser Substance spread on the ground to make the soil richer.

Fresh water Water that is drinkable and not salty like the sea.

Gravity The force that pulls things down towards the ground.

Groundwater Water held in the soil or in between rock.

Insulation To cover something with material in order to stop heat escaping from it.

Landfill site A place where waste materials are buried and covered over with soil.

Maintenance The work done to keep something in good condition.

Particles Tiny parts of something.

Pollutants Substances that are harmful and poisonous to the environment.

Polystyrene A light, stiff plastic used to make packaging and insulation.

Septic tank An underground tank in which sewage is collected.

Sewage Liquid and solid waste that is carried away in sewers and drains.

Sludge Soft, thick mud.

Toxic Poisonous.

Washer A rubber ring that acts as a seal to stop a tap leaking.

Well A hole from which you can draw water from under the ground.

Further information

Books

A Glass of Water (The Science In), Anna Claybourne, 2008 (Franklin Watts)

Waste Water (Dealing with Waste), Sally Morgan, 2006 (Franklin Watts)

Water (What Happens When We Recycle?), Jillian Powell, 2009 (Franklin Watts)

Water (Read and Learn: What Living Things Need), Vicky Parker, 2006 (Raintree)

The Water Cycle (Nature's Cycles), Sally Morgan, 2008 (Wayland)

Websites

www.niwater.com/education
This educational site includes animations of how the water cycle and water treatment works.

www.water-guide.org.uk
Here you can find out all about the water industry and the companies that work within it. It also includes tips on how to save water.

www.dwi.gov.uk/children/welcome.htm
This site shows you how vital water is to us all. It also has more information on how water is collected and cleaned after it has been used.

Note to parents and teachers: Every effort has been made by the Publishers to ensure that these websites are suitable for children, that they are of the highest educational value, and that they contain no inappropriate or offensive material. However, because of the nature of the Internet, it is impossible to guarantee that the contents of these sites will not be altered. We strongly advise that Internet access is supervised by a responsible adult.

Index